Praise for *Roll into a Perfectly Made Bed*

"Rebecca at Down Etc is the best! Highest quality, great consultant, fantastic prices, super-fast delivery. She has beautifully handled several bedrooms and bathrooms in three separate residences."

—**Jason Beghe, film and television actor**

"*Roll into a Perfectly Made Bed*—a great read! Finally Rebecca brings her expertise and passion to educate us about the art of the bed. She has clear diagrams to get us to understand the basics and perfect tips you can implement immediately to enhance your personal or guests' quality of sleep. We spend a third of our life in bed. Although sleep seems so simple, it has become incredibly complicated over the years. Our 24/7 electronic worlds are creating more havoc in clearing our minds at the end of each day. More and more people are having trouble getting to sleep or actually staying asleep. Prescription sleep aids have been on the rise. Rebecca's insights can help one understand how to set up the optimal setting to create the proper atmosphere for a great night's sleep. It's a must-read if you're looking to understand the importance of refining a few things to create a perfect atmosphere around sleep!"

—**Lorraine Francis, AIA, LEED, BD+C, regional director of hospitality interiors, associate, Gensler**

"In my ever-changing daily life, I realize I have limited control of external factors. The most important aspect of having a productive day actually starts the day before by getting a good night's sleep. It may seem simple, but be sure to rest as long as your body/mind needs. This book will help you create the bedroom environment necessary to achieve the rest you need to get a great start to your day and a head start on everybody else."

—**Michael B. Hoffmann, general manager, Inn at Perry Cabin**

"As an avid traveler and someone who is constantly on the road, I truly value being in my own bed. Since buying the Down Etc. pillows, my sleep has never been the same as they provide me with the comfort and support I need to wake up well rested. Thus, I continue to recommend these pillows to all my friends and family."

—**Scott Menke, chief executive officer, Paragon Gaming**

"Attention to detail is necessary to provide a world-class hotel experience. We have been able to provide that experience using the kind of expertise and attention to detail included in this book."

—Joel Moore, vice president of hotel operations, Thunder Valley Casino Resort

"This book exemplifies my experience in dealing with Rebecca that there is no detail too small when it comes to creating a bed that will provide our guests with a great night's sleep and a memorable stay."

—Dick Moskal, vice president of purchasing, Affinity Gaming

"If your bedding is well-designed and constructed, delivered on time and as specified, offers the aesthetic attributes your guests readily recognize and appreciate, while at the same time providing your operators with superior product performance metrics, it probably has a Down Etc label attached to it."

—Tony Reiss, director of project services, Hilton

"Rebecca Litwin has captured her passion to provide a great night's sleep in *Roll Into a Perfectly Made Bed*. As my colleague and mentor for over a decade, I can attest to Rebecca's belief in the art of making a bed. In this book, she makes that art available to everyone."

—Katie Reuland, director of operations, Down Etc

"A great night's sleep is more than a motto for Rebecca Litwin and Down Etc; it's a mission. In this primer on the art of bed making, a leading supplier to the best hotels around the world outlines in words and pictures everything necessary to create the bed you want to jump into, whether you're at home or away. I will be certain it is kept within easy reach of the housekeepers in all of our properties."

—Rick Riess, vice president, Montage Hotels & Resorts; managing director, Montage Laguna Beach

"For fifteen years, Rebecca and the Down Etc team have shared with me their knowledge, experience, and enthusiasm for creating the bedding necessary to provide hotel guests with a memorable experience. This book reflects the 'can do" attitude and commitment to providing the perfect bedding for each project that have made me a fan now and in the future."

—Terri Shearer, partner, Filament Hospitality

"*Roll into a Perfectly Made Bed* is a must-read for anyone wishing to create their own perfect sleep environment at home. Rebecca Litwin offers a straightforward, intuitive, step-by-step framework in this savvy 'insider's tool of the trade.' Read this book if you wish to bring the delightful sleep experience enjoyed at the world's best hotels into the bedrooms of you and your guests."

—Polina Steier, editor-in-chief, *Caviar Affair* magazine

"Rebecca Litwin taught me more about beds, pillows, featherbeds, duvet covers, and all other issues of sleeping comfort in twenty-four hours that I learned in a career of forty years. She is my go-to expert and the only woman I know who has figured out how to keep down feathers where they belong!"

—Roger Thomas, executive vice president, design, Wynn Design and Development

"In this book, Rebecca and Down Etc share their excitement and the knowledge of top of the bed products, which has made them invaluable collaborators in bringing our creative visions and design concepts to life for our hotels. This book affirms their ability to balance style and substance to create a beautiful sleep experience for everyone."

—Sabine Vessnow, director, development–sourcing, Sydell Group

ROLL INTO A PERFECTLY MADE *Bed*

ALL YOU NEED TO KNOW ABOUT THE ART OF BEDMAKING

by down etc

Notes from a bedmaking journey

Published by Advantage, Charleston, South Carolina.
Member of Advantage Media Group.

ADVANTAGE is a registered trademark, and the Advantage colophon is a trademark of Advantage Media Group, Inc.

Printed in the United States of America.

Cover photograph by Peter Sukonik.

10 9 8 7 6 5 4 3 2 1

ISBN: 978-1-59932-876-8
LCCN: 2017951051

This publication is designed to provide accurate and authoritative information in regard to the subject matter covered. It is sold with the understanding that the publisher is not engaged in rendering legal, accounting, or other professional services. If legal advice or other expert assistance is required, the services of a competent professional person should be sought.

Advantage Media Group is proud to be a part of the Tree Neutral® program. Tree Neutral offsets the number of trees consumed in the production and printing of this book by taking proactive steps such as planting trees in direct proportion to the number of trees used to print books. To learn more about Tree Neutral, please visit www.treeneutral.com.

Advantage Media Group is a publisher of business, self-improvement, and professional development books. We help entrepreneurs, business leaders, and professionals share their Stories, Passion, and Knowledge to help others Learn & Grow. Do you have a manuscript or book idea that you would like us to consider for publishing? Please visit advantagefamily.com or call 1.866.775.1696.

CONTENTS

Notes from a bedmaking journey

*A*CKNOWLEDGMENTS: Thank you. Merci. Gracias. Danke. Salamaat. Xie Xie. Arigato.

Thank you for embarking on this journey of bed making! We hope you enjoy it as much as we have enjoyed sharing our thoughts on how to make bed making easier and more fun.

We owe our thanks to the numerous housekeepers who inspired us to embark on this journey, which we have wanted to take for so long. Thanks to the following people:

- Our parents, who taught us to make our beds correctly.
- Our families, for their unconditional love.
- Our graphic artists, for their continued support and encouragement.
- Our publisher, for their patience and unstinted support.
- Our office staff, for proofreading our thoughts.
- All our clients and dear bed making professionals—we could never do your jobs as well as you do.
- Finally, our housekeeping divas, for helping us publish this story and for sharing your passion with housekeepers all over this wonderful universe.

We wish you *a great night's sleep* in **a perfectly made bed**.

Rebecca Litwin

down etc ▴▪•

www.downetc.com
info@downetc.com
1-866-downetc (369-6382)

Notes from a bedmaking journey

INTRODUCTION

FOR EVERYONE from the weary traveler staying overnight at a hotel to the exhausted worker trying to catch up on sleep at home, nothing is more frustrating than a poorly made bed. We all require a quality pillow and a properly made bed with clean, crisp linens to facilitate *a great night's sleep*. And though we may be comfortable in our beds at home, getting *a great night's sleep* when on the road or during vacation is like winning the jackpot. Too often, I hear travelers criticize hotels for having lousy beds, unkempt bedding, and uncomfortable mattresses unsuitable for their patrons.

Because we are taught to make our own beds growing up, we expect something fancy, different, and exciting when we check into a hotel—a wow factor that transforms the stay into a memorable experience. In hotels around the world, a well-made bed is both an important tradition and a design standard.

"If you want to change the world, start off by making your bed." This was the first of ten life lessons identified by US Navy Admiral William H. McRaven in his commencement address to the graduating class at the University of Texas at Austin on May 17, 2014. I could not agree more.

I wrote this book for the workers around the world who make beds every day for a living, as well as for the homemakers who make beds every day for their families. I firmly believe *a great night's sleep* is the best medicine for the tired body, soul, and mind. After years of accumulating knowledge on the subject, I have finally put my thoughts on paper so that the generations to come can benefit from my expertise on how to achieve the perfectly made bed.

A perfectly made bed is particularly important for those in the hospitality industry, where there are standards of cleanliness and order that must be met. At home, you have the choice of making your own bed however you like, in whatever way works best for you. A perfectly made bed is not necessary for a great night's sleep—though I share some tips here that will certainly improve the quality of your sleep.

There are many components that add value to a bed, and I discuss each component in the following chapters. I also provide a glossary of terms at the back of the book.

It gives me great pleasure to share my ideas and values with you, dear reader, whether you are a room attendant, a housekeeper, or simply someone interested in the intricate art of bed making. I hope this book makes your life at least a little easier. Thank you for joining me on this journey toward making a perfect bed for your guests, your loved ones, and yourself.

CHAPTER

1

TYPES OF BEDS, BED FRAMES, HEADBOARDS, MATTRESSES & BOX SPRINGS

TYPES OF BEDS

There are various types of beds; the number-one criterion when selecting a bed is the size of the bedroom. A bed should never feel crammed into a room. When deciding where to position the bed, it is important to consider the juxtaposition of the size of room, the ceiling height, the nightstand, the headboard, and the height of the bed.

Types of beds include:

- bunk bed (with or without the trundle)
- crib
- twin
- full/double
- queen
- king (California king or Eastern king)
- daybed
- pullout sofa
- in-wall bed

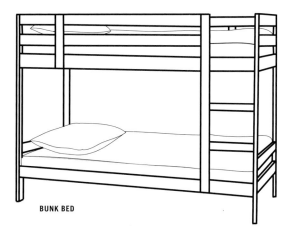

BUNK BED

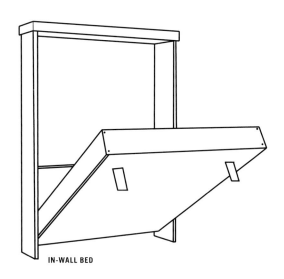

IN-WALL BED

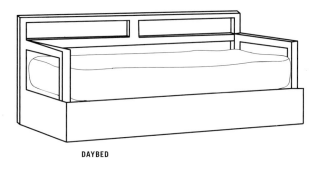

DAYBED

■ rollaway (cot)

In hotels where families visit frequently, it is common to sleep five persons in a room. This is where the bunk bed comes in handy. A family of five does not need to rent a second room, as they will select a queen or king bed with a bunk bed that sleeps three children. A family with one child can select a king or queen with a pullout sofa bed (or daybed). During the daytime, the bed is used as a sofa. At turndown (evening housekeeping service), the sofa is transformed into a bed.

PLATFORM BED

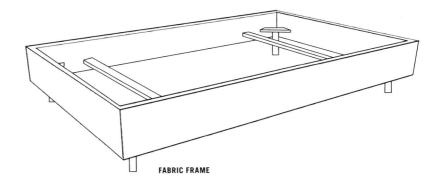

FABRIC FRAME

THE BED FRAME

One of the main components of a bed is the bed frame. There are many different kinds of frames: those built for a pedestal bed, a platform bed, or just a conventional bed. When you select a bed frame, it needs to be able to hold the weight of the box spring and the mattress. If you select a bed without a frame that has slats underneath the bed, you may want to place a bed board—a flat piece of wood—on top of the slats and underneath the mattress in order to give the bed a firmer, more comfortable feel.

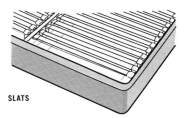

SLATS

The optimal height of the bed frame is entirely up to you, but some vital things to consider when making the decision are:

- Can a vacuum fit under the bed for easy cleaning of the carpet underneath?
- When you sit at the edge of the bed, can you stand up with ease?
- When you make the bed, do you have to bend too far?
- When you lie on the bed, is it too high?

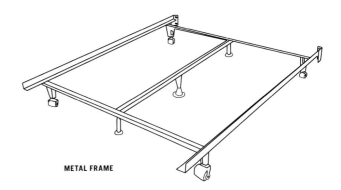

METAL FRAME

Because bed frames collect dust, they will need to be cleaned, which is not easy. This is a task that should be added to your cleaning schedule. In a typical hotel, a bed frame is cleaned every time the mattress and box spring are rotated. Be sure the bed frame is correctly placed with all of the legs touching the floor; they should be firm and accurately aligned. If even one leg does not rest completely on the ground, your bed is not positioned well.

A bed frame should be changed every time you replace the mattress and box spring, which are changed according to their wear and tear. In the hospitality industry, the frequency of occupancy drives the replacement schedule. Typically, the cycle can be anywhere from four to six years.

WOOD OR METAL

VINYL OR FABRIC

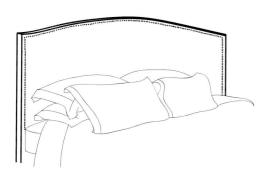

LEATHER OR LEATHERETTE

PADDED FABRIC

THE HEADBOARD

There are various types of headboards. They are typically made of wood and enhanced with fabric padding for a luxurious look. Headboards are either mounted to the wall behind the bed or attached to the bed frame. It is imperative that the headboard be cleaned at every checkout. Typically, when a room is deep-cleaned, the headboard is removed from the wall and cleaned, front and back. Should you find any insects behind the headboard, follow your hotel's pest control procedures.

THE MATTRESS AND BOX SPRING

When selecting a mattress and box spring, the following factors will influence the quality and price of the product:

- size
- ticking (the fabric)
- coil count
- coil gauge (the smaller the gauge, the thicker the coil)
- stitching
- fill
- order quantity

MATTRESS SELECTIONS
(SIDE VIEW)

TWIN 39" W x 76" L

FULL 54" W x 76" L

QUEEN 60" W x 80" L

CONTRACT KING 72" W x 80" L

KING 78" W x 80" L

CALIFORNIA KING 72" W x 84" L

THE MATTRESS

In recent years, the hospitality industry has shifted toward a preference for pillow top mattresses. This has made bed making even more difficult, since tucking the sheets in around a bed can be tedious. For this reason, sheets must be the right size. When selecting a new mattress, make sure your existing sheets fit, as they may have been sized for a thinner mattress or shrunk from repeated washing. (For more information about the sizing of sheets, please see chapter 3.)

Make sure your mattress is comfortable, durable, and easily cleaned. Whenever a hotel room or bedroom at home is deep-cleaned, it is best to also shampoo the mattress (similar to shampooing an upholstered sofa, chair, or carpet) in order to remove any dirt and dust that has gathered there over time. If a mattress has been stained with blood or infected with bedbugs, both the mattress and box spring should be completely destroyed to avoid continued contamination. When installing beds for a new hotel, it is wise to use mattress encasements, as they help prevent the mattresses from getting stained, thus extending their lifetime. Since encasements sometimes make the bed warmer, it is important to select the right breathable fabric and to utilize mattress toppers and/or pads. (For more about mattress encasements, toppers, and pads, please see chapter 2.)

THE BOX SPRING

The box spring is the foundation for a bed. The size of a box spring should match the size of the mattress selected. The box spring is designed to carry the weight of the mattress; typically, split box springs (two units) are used under a king mattress.

SOFA BED OR ROLLAWAY BED

The height of the mattress and box spring in sofa beds and rollaway beds varies according to the brand and design of the beds. Typically, a sofa bed has a mattress that is easily folded.

For a fancy rollaway bed, you can make a custom rollaway with a higher headboard and a replaceable fabric headboard cover. Use a rollaway cover when storing the bed upright to maintain cleanliness when not in use.

Should you need an even fancier rollaway bed, try a custom bed skirt!

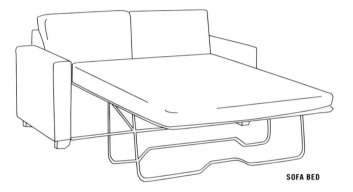

SOFA BED

FOLDING ROLLAWAY BED

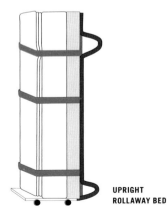

UPRIGHT ROLLAWAY BED

Notes from a bedmaking journey

*T*HE MATTRESS TOPPER PROVIDES an additional layer of comfort, while the mattress pad provides extra protection against stains and soil. Selected and used together properly, they will help you achieve the level of comfort and cleanliness desired for your bed, whether at home or away. However, the best protection you can provide for your mattress and box spring are encasements.

WHAT ARE MATTRESS AND BOX SPRING ENCASEMENTS?

Box springs and mattresses are major investments that should be protected. Bedbugs are a public health pest due to their ability to travel between your hotel and your home in luggage and on clothing. Encasing your mattress and box spring, as well as your pillows, in a protective cover is your first precaution against infestation.

The onguard!® fitted encasement zips around your mattress and box spring to create a breathable and moisture absorbent barrier to bedbugs. Encasements are sized according to the size of your mattress and box spring:

- twin: 39" x 76" x 12"

- full: 54" x 75" x 12"
- queen: 60" x 80" x 15"
- king: 78" x 80" x 15"
- California king: 75" x 86" x 15"

Bedbug problems create the perception that your hotel and home are not clean. One poor experience can cause a broad ripple effect on a hotel or hotel group. Avoid this bad perception.

WHY USE MATTRESS TOPPERS?

Mattress toppers provide an extra layer of cushion when placed directly on top of the mattress. Construction and materials used in mattress toppers vary according to preference. Some of the options available include:

FEATHERBED TOPPERS: Featherbed toppers are luxurious and make for an extremely cozy bed. Like comforters/duvets, featherbed toppers utilize down and feathers blown between layers of fabric sewn together with a baffled box construction designed to keep the feathers in place. Like all down and feather products, featherbed toppers need to breathe, and fluffing or shaking the featherbed toppers several times a week is recommended to ensure the feathers maintain their maximum loft.

POLYESTER TOPPERS: Unlike featherbed toppers, polyester toppers utilize a polyester fill. These toppers require less fluffing; however, they do increase warmth, as they do not breathe as well as featherbed toppers. Like featherbed toppers, polyester toppers are composed of layers of fabric sewn together with a baffled box construction to keep the interior material in place.

MEMORY FOAM TOPPERS: Memory foam is a popular material for toppers, as many people like its ability to mold to the body's contours and relieve pressure. Memory foam toppers typically measure two to four inches in thickness. Although memory foam can increase warmth, this warmth can be reduced through the use of breathable open-celled foam, which provides ventilation that wicks away body heat and moisture for a comfortable but hygienic sleeping environment.

MEMORY FOAM COOL GEL TOPPERS: Like the classic memory foam toppers, these toppers provide comfort by molding to the sleeper's body. The addition of gel further relieves pressure while reducing warmth.

COTTON TOPPERS: Cotton mattress toppers are constructed with layers of cotton to provide a light and durable cushion, as well as further protection for the mattress.

WOOL TOPPERS: Wool toppers utilize a layer of wool between layers of fabric sewn together, designed to keep the layers in place. Wool toppers are usually antimicrobial and antibacterial, making them the choice for allergy sufferers. The moisture-wicking properties of wool also make it a terrific material to sleep on.

LATEX TOPPERS: The best quality latex toppers are constructed similarly to other mattress toppers utilizing a layer of organic rubber between layers of fabric sewn together.

WHY USE MATTRESS PADS?

Mattresses are susceptible to numerous contaminants ranging from bodily excretions like sweat and drool to accidental spills of food and drink. An unprotected mattress can be easily ruined. In addition to protecting mattresses from such contaminants, full-coverage mattress pads can protect mattresses from bedbug infestations, and waterproof mattress pads can reduce the possibility of mold growth resulting from moisture reaching the mattress.

A mattress pad is not as thick as a mattress topper and is most often made of quilted cotton or synthetic material. The mattress pad goes over the mattress topper. While a mattress topper might lie loosely on top of the mattress, the mattress pad is typically constructed with either a skirt that will surround the mattress on all sides like a fitted sheet or bands to anchor the mattress pad in place.

We recommend a mattress pad with a 100 percent cotton top layer, as this improves the pad's breathability and prevents damage to the bottom sheet directly on top of the pad. The mattress pad should be laundered at the end of each guest's stay unless it becomes soiled, in which case it should be laundered immediately.

STYLES AND MATERIALS:
Mattress pads come in a number of styles, including:

- a flat mattress pad
- a flat mattress pad with anchor bands
- a flat mattress pad with a fitted skirt, also known as a bed sac, which surrounds the mattress like a fitted sheet
- a Lily Pads® mattress pad, which is a waterproof mattress pad that is also motionless, noiseless, and breathable. Lily Pads® mattress pads can be manufactured with or without anchor bands or fitted skirts

Mattress pads can be manufactured in a number of different materials, including:

- quilted sheeting
- memory foam
- egg-crate foam
- down and feathers
- other materials including cotton, wool, polyester,

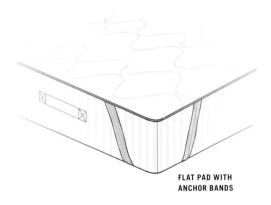

FLAT PAD WITH ANCHOR BANDS

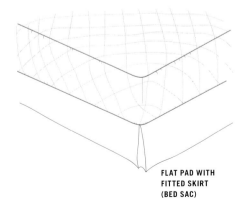

FLAT PAD WITH FITTED SKIRT (BED SAC)

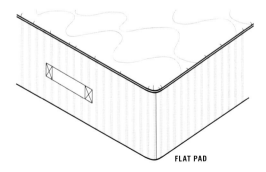

FLAT PAD

silk, woodpulp, and latex

WHAT TO CONSIDER WHEN SELECTING AND MAINTAINING MATTRESS TOPPERS AND MATTRESS PADS:

Comfort is the key factor. You want to choose a mattress topper and mattress pad that will provide cushion and protection, without retaining too much warmth. This requires you to consider both the fabric and the fill used in construction. You also want to choose a style and material that will allow the mattress topper and mattress pad to remain in place but quiet while in use.

Maintenance and durability come next. You will want to consider how well the mattress topper and mattress pad you choose will wear, as well as what will be required for laundering. As with pillows and comforters/duvets, we recommend protectors be used on down and feather toppers. All mattress toppers should be removed for cleaning as needed. As mattress toppers are large and can only be dry-cleaned or washed in an industrial machine, we recommend placing the mattress pad on top of the mattress topper.

Size will depend on your mattress. As both the mattress topper and mattress pad should provide full coverage for the top of the mattress, they are available in sizes to correspond to mattress sizes. For example:

- twin: 39" W x 76" L
- full: 54" W x 76" L
- queen: 60" W x 80" L
- contract King: 72" W x 80" L
- king: 78" W x 80" L
- California king: 72" W x 84" L

THE QUALITY OF LINEN FABRIC is determined by the thread count (TC) and yarn size. The TC is measured by the number of stitches in a one-inch square of fabric. The higher the TC, the softer (hence, fancier) the quality of linen. For your home, you can select anywhere from 180 TC to 600 TC. High-quality linens with high thread counts play a large part in a hotel's ratings.

When choosing and purchasing linens for a hotel, you must take the following into account:

- Your laundry facility and the method of laundering, including whether you have onsite or offsite laundry facilities and whether a flat iron (mangle) is utilized. This will determine your laundering costs, as well as the necessary number of par.

- Your budget.

- Types of linens and fabrics, which can be a blend of cotton and polyester or all cotton.

- The life of the linens, which determines the number of washes they can undergo.

- How you will store the linens and how you will place them on housekeeping carts.

- Whether your hotel is located in a high- or low-soil area.

- The demographics of your hotel's guests, their uses and activities.

TYPES OF LINENS:

- pillowcase: open sack, overlay closure, buttons, zippers, ties, or flanged
- fitted sheet
- flat sheet (bottom, second, or top)
- decorative top sheet
- coverlet
- comforter/duvet cover: open sack, overlay closure, buttons, or ties

LINEN SIZE:

The size of the linens is crucial for a bed to be made correctly. The length and width of the sheets will depend on the size of the bed. The size of the comforter/duvet is a design decision based on the desired drop. Covers are determined by the size of the comforter/duvet.

The sheets used to make a bed need to be the right size. A king sheet must be used on a king bed and a queen sheet on a queen bed. Trying to save money by using a queen sheet on a king bed will not work, as the sheet will not cover the entire mattress on all four sides. The reverse is also problematic: When you use a king sheet on a queen bed, it will take longer for the housekeeper to make the bed. In addition, you will waste money by paying more for the purchase and laundering of a king sheet.

In homes, fitted sheets are common. Though some hotels have also adopted them, the downside of fitted sheets is that the creases are difficult to iron out in commercial laundry facilities. In addition, the elastic around fitted sheets tends to stretch over frequent washes, rendering the sheets ill-fitting and their appearance off-design. For both homes and hotels that use fitted sheets, it is important to select a size that accurately fits all four sides of the mattress.

Home Tip: Wash your linens together and separately from towels and other laundry for maximum efficiency.

LINEN STORAGE:

The linens, stored in hampers or bins or stacked on shelves, should be neatly placed. Bins holding clean linens should not be used to hold soiled linens. If you have to use a soiled linen bin to hold clean linens, make sure the bins are disinfected and cleaned prior to use. Minimum handling of the linens is best.

When storing linens on closet shelves, use the FIFO (first in first out) method for rotation of inventory. Rotate the linens at the bottom to the top when placing new linens away, and place the new linens at the bottom. Once washed, linens should be allowed to breathe.

THE LIFE OF THE LINENS DEPENDS ON:

- number of washes
- wear and tear
- handling at the laundry facility
- handling at the hotel (in carts, linen hampers, linen closets, on shelves, etc.)
- number of par in circulation
- quality of the mattress pad (made of non-pilling poly-cotton or cotton fabric)

WHAT IS PAR?

A single par describes the number of sheets by type and size it takes to cover all the beds in a hotel. The number of par maintained by a hotel depends on whether it has an onsite or offsite laundry facility. Typically, three par of linens should suffice for an onsite laundry facility. If the laundry is done offsite, you will need four par.

- First par is in the guest room.

- Second par is on the cart or in the linen closet.

- Third par is the soiled linen being laundered.

- Fourth par is the cleaned linen on the way to the hotel from an off-site laundry facility.

If you have a green program, you will need fewer par.

BEDSHEET DISTRIBUTIONS

The top sheet is the last sheet you use to make the bed. The bedsheet distributions per style of bed making are as follows:

- Three sheets with blanket* (called triple-sheeting): Bottom sheet/second sheet/blanket/top sheet.

- Two sheets with blanket*: Bottom sheet/top sheet/blanket.

- Two sheets with comforter/duvet: Bottom sheet/top sheet/duvet in a cover.

- One sheet with comforter/duvet (European style): Bottom sheet/duvet in a cover.

* Blanket could be feather, down, or hypoallergenic polyester.

TIME SAVERS

In hotels, to make the bed making process fast and easy, it is important to have the thread colors on the hem of the sheet correlate with the size of the sheet. Once you open your hotel and decide on the color of the thread, make sure your linen vendor does not change the color. The common thread colors for the hem are red for king sheets, green for queen sheets, and blue for twin sheets. Woven, sewn-in labels can also be color-coded by sheet type or size. Once a housekeeper is trained in a method, it is best to stick to it!

Another time-saving suggestion is a two-inch finished hem at the top and bottom of the flat sheets so that they may be placed on the bed in either direction. For additional efficiency, keep the bottom and top sheet in the same style to avoid multiple items in inventory.

At home, you can make things easier by having different size sheets in different colors or by storing sheets on shelves according to size.

CHAPTER

4

PILLOWS

"A PILLOW IS THE
PERFECT ACCENT TO
EVERY ROOM"
—down etc

PERFECT PILLOW is one of the answers to *a great night's sleep*. Choosing the correct pillow, decorative or sleeping, is a matter of personal preference. In the hospitality industry, it is important also to consider the type of hotel and overall design of the room. The Pillow Butler® system is an essential way to ensure that all of your guests get *a great night's sleep*, as it will allow each guest to find the appropriate pillow. (For more about the Pillow Butler® system, please see chapter 5.)

PILLOW SIZE

Dimensions of sleeping pillows include:

- king size: 20'' W x 36'' L
- queen size: 20'' W X 30'' L
- standard size: 20'' W x 26'' L
- Euro: 26'' W x 26'' L
- boudoir: 12'' W x 16'' L
- decorative: various sizes

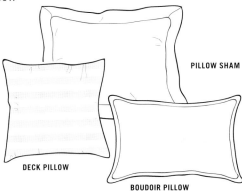

PILLOW SHAM

DECK PILLOW

BOUDOIR PILLOW

It is recommended that all decorative pillows have removable covers that can be washed at every checkout to ensure hygienic beds.

PILLOW FILL

The following are some of the options for pillow fill:

- goose feathers
- goose down
- duck feathers
- duck down
- silk
- polyester
- buckwheat
- wool
- cotton
- kapok
- memory foam
- gel
- latex

When selecting a pillow fill, take into consideration the outside temperature, as well as the interior temperature of the bedroom, to allow maximum air circulation for a comfortable sleep.

STANDARD PILLOW PRACTICES

A king pillow is typically used on a king bed and a queen pillow on a queen bed. Standard pillows are used on double beds, bunk beds, and rollaway beds. Alternatively, a hotel might choose to use all standard pillows or all king pillows. Pillow practices are left to the hotel standards, design aesthetics, and budget. However, one practice that is not optional is the use of pillow protectors, which should be used on every pillow.

LUXURY IS USUALLY DEFINED AS FOUR TO SIX PILLOWS ON THE BED:

- King bed: Two soft king pillows, two firm king pillows, and two Euro squares on the bed. In addition, two hypoallergenic polyester pillows in the closet in a PVC bag or closet box.
- Queen/double bed: Two soft queen pillows, two firm queen pillows, and two Euro squares on the bed. In addition, two hypoallergenic polyester pillows in the closet in a PVC bag or closet box.

READY TO WEAR IS USUALLY DEFINED AS TWO TO FOUR PILLOWS ON THE BED:

- King bed: Two firm king pillows and possibly two Euro squares on the bed. In addition, two hypoallergenic polyester pillows in the closet in a PVC bag or closet box.
- Queen bed: Two firm queen pillows and possibly two Euro squares on the bed. In addition, two hypoallergenic polyester pillows in the closet in a PVC bag or closet box.

ECONOMICAL IS USUALLY DEFINED AS TWO PILLOWS ON THE BED:

- King bed: Two firm standard pillows. In addition, one hypoallergenic polyester pillow in the closet in a PVC bag.

- Queen bed: Two firm standard pillows. In addition, one hypoallergenic polyester pillow in the closet in a PVC bag.

PVC CLOSET BAG

CLOSET BOX

Home Tip: For your pillows at home, put them in the dryer every couple of weeks for just four or five minutes to open up the down or other fill. You sleep on them every night, packing the fill down. A few minutes in the dryer, and your pillow will come back fluffy and refreshed. This is the same reason we fluff pillows—allowing air to flow through the fabric and the fill just gives them a fresher and cleaner feel.

PILLOW HYGIENE PRACTICE

Always use a pillow protector! The embarrassing truth is that we all drool at night when we sleep. Pillow protectors come with a regular or invisible zipper. We highly recommend the use of pillow protectors for both home and hotel use, as these protectors are washable and are also an effective barrier against dirt. When you change pillowcases, check your pillow protectors. If there are stains or odors, the pillow protectors should be washed. Be sure to close any zippers before laundering. For impeccable cleanliness, decorative pillows need to have removable covers for easy laundering.

For hotels, the best hygienic practice is to replace or change every pillowcase (pillow slip) on a sleeping pillow or a decorative pillow when a guest checks out. If you cannot afford this laundry cost, avoid the decorative pillows! Your productivity requirements will dictate this process. Travelers are smart, educated, and well informed in regard to the cleaning procedures in the hospitality industry. Today's culture provides quick access to public review and complaint websites. It is easier than ever for guests to relay every thought and frustration to the rest of the public. This can hinder your hotel's ability to thrive. Cleanliness is the basis of the hospitality industry, and it is our responsibility every day.

CHOOSING THE RIGHT COVERS

The pillowcase is an important piece of the bed. The criteria to consider when selecting a pillowcase include:

- Budget: Unit price/Desired number of par
- Fabric (cotton, polyester, combined cotton, etc.)
- Thread count (TC)
- Size
- Style (flange, open sack, and overlay closures)
- Design and color of the fabric
- Laundering requirements
- Life of the product

When selecting pillowcases with a flange, remember that they will need special attention with the ironing process. This will increase your laundering costs.

DO'S AND DON'TS

When placing a pillow in a pillowcase, place the pillowcase on the bed and insert the pillow into the case. Never hold the pillowcase under your chin. The pillowcase should never touch your uniform. Try to keep the pillowcase as clean as possible without any cross-contamination.

Another way to insert the pillow already in its protector into its pillowcase is by rolling down the sides of the pillowcase so as to form the base of a well. Set the pillow in the center of the well and then lift the sides of the pillowcase up the pillow.

DECORATIVE PILLOW TALK

When a guest walks into a guest room, the first thing that catches his or her eye is a beautiful bed. The decorative pillows in many hotels are used mainly to enhance the look of the top of the bed and the room—and they do; however, they also increase the workload when making a bed. Ideally, use covers that can be washed after every checkout in order to maintain maximum cleanliness. Decorative pillows come in any number of shapes and sizes.

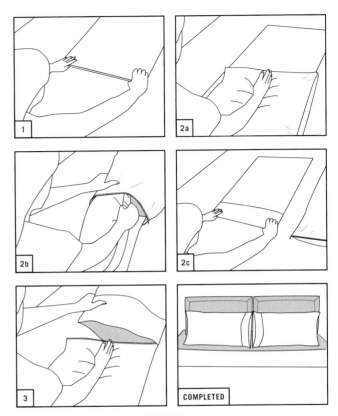

PILLOW PREPARATION

STEP 1: Lay the pillow protector on the bed. Do not hold it against uniform.

STEP 2: a) Karate chop the pillow lengthwise. b) Hold with one hand and insert into pillow protector. c) Close pillow protector.

STEP 3: Repeat STEPS 1 and 2 to insert the pillow into the pillowcase.

COMPLETED: When placing the pillows on the bed, the open edges of the pillowcases should face one another in the center of the bed.

Notes from a bedmaking journey

*W*HAT WOULD IT BE LIKE if you could, at the touch of a button, summon a Pillow Butler® who would assess the needs of your sleeper and then select and provide the perfect pillow to meet those needs?

Pillow Butler® service can be introduced at your hotel to help every guest find the best pillow for them to sleep on. The Pillow Butler® is a pillow storage and delivery system; it provides guests with a menu of pillows, it helps the staff understand the different questions to ask in order to help guests determine what pillow would be best for them for a great night's sleep, and finally it serves up exactly the right pillow from your collection.

EVOLUTION OF PILLOW SERVICE

Your guests do not want more of the standard-issue pillow; they want a variety of pillows from which to choose. Pillow menus and services have become more than a novelty—they have become the new standard in sleep luxury for many high-end hotels around the world. Guests can often miss the comforts of home when staying in anonymous hotel rooms. Offering a pillow menu and a full Pillow Butler® service will provide guests with the comforts of home by supplying them with pillows of their own choosing!

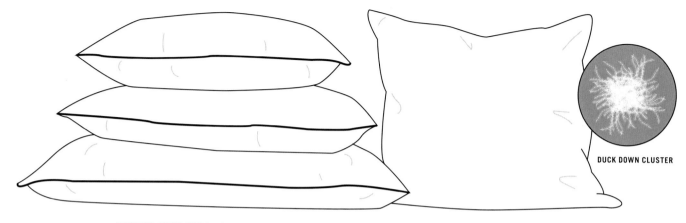

STANDARD, QUEEN, KING PILLOW

EURO SQUARE PILLOW

DUCK DOWN CLUSTER

A Pillow Butler® BEGINS BY ASSESSING EACH GUEST'S PILLOW NEEDS.
Each guest will have certain preferences with respect to pillows. Some of the questions you might pose to assist each guest in selecting from the offerings of your pillow menu include:

- In which position do you sleep (side, back, or stomach)?
- Do you snore?
- Do you have allergies?
- Do you prefer organic and natural products?
- What size and fill do you prefer?
- Would you enjoy a luxury treatment such as aromatherapy?

There are many factors to consider. For example, a pregnant woman might choose a body pillow while a child might delight in a boudoir pillow, which is just the right size for a child's head or a child's hug. As a Pillow Butler®, don't forget to consider the height and weight of your guests.

OPTIONS TO CONSIDER:

ALL WHITE GOOSE DOWN: The softest of all white goose down pillows. This pillow will gently cradle the neck as the sleeper dreams.

50 PERCENT WHITE GOOSE DOWN/50 PERCENT WHITE GOOSE FEATHER: The perfect blend of down and feathers to provide a tranquil sleep and subtle neck support.

25 PERCENT WHITE GOOSE DOWN/75 PERCENT WHITE GOOSE FEATHER: This pillow provides medium support appropriate for all sleep positions.

RHAPSODY WRAP: This is the firmest sleeping pillow. It contains a feather core to provide extra support for the neck while sleeping or extra support for the back while sitting up in bed. The core is surrounded by a 30 percent down / 70 percent feather wrap for softness.

DIAMOND SUPPORT® FEATHER: The firmest of all feather pillows is well suited for snorers or to provide support to sleepers with heavy musculature.

AQUAPLUSH® HYPOALLERGENIC: This polyester alternative to a down pillow will have the sleeper wondering if it is not really down. These pillows are available in soft or firm fills.

BODY PILLOW: This pillow is typically twenty by sixty inches in size. It is available in a variety of fills and provides a full body hug.

LOVE PILLOW: This twenty-by-sixty-inch body pillow is contoured to fit the body. It is excellent for side sleepers or couples sharing a pillow.

BUCKWHEAT PILLOW: Filled with 100 percent buckwheat hulls, this pillow is used by sleepers with body aches and pains, sleeplessness, and snoring.

ORGANIC WOOL PILLOW: For a night of conscientious luxury, choose this 100 percent certified organic Merino wool–filled pillow with fabric ticking.

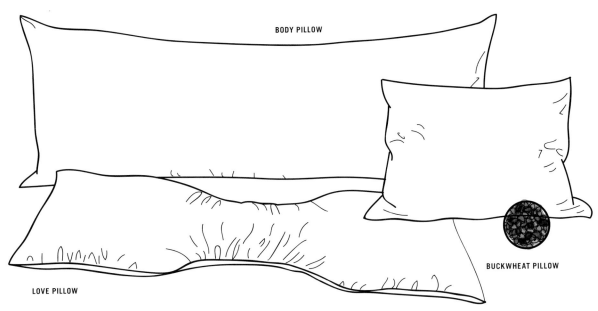

BODY PILLOW

BUCKWHEAT PILLOW

LOVE PILLOW

TRAVEL PILLOW

BOLSTER: With fill comprised of a blend of down and feathers, this pillow provides support for the neck, lower back, and/or knees. It is available in a variety of fills and sizes.

BOUDOIR PILLOW: This perfect little pillow is twelve by sixteen inches and filled with all white goose down. Choose this pillow for a snug little hug while sleeping or traveling.

MUSIC PILLOW: These contain small speakers that can be connected to your MP3 player.

MEMORY FOAM CONTOUR PILLOW: Memory foam pillows contour to support the head and neck to relieve pressure.

MASSAGE PILLOW: Contains a unique particle surface designed to massage the acupressure points of the head while sleeping.

FOOT WRAP PILLOW: Gently supports the ankles to relieve leg fatigue and eliminate pressure on the foot.

LEG WEDGE PILLOW: Gently supports the ankles to relieve leg fatigue and support the upper back during sleep.

GEL PILLOW: Provides a cool and refreshing gel layer over a memory foam, polyester, or down and feather pillow. Cradles the head, neck, and shoulders.

AROMATHERAPY PILLOW: A cotton or silk pillowcase from the Tiara Silks® collection, containing a sachet of soothing herbs tucked into a hidden pocket, will soothe your sleep.

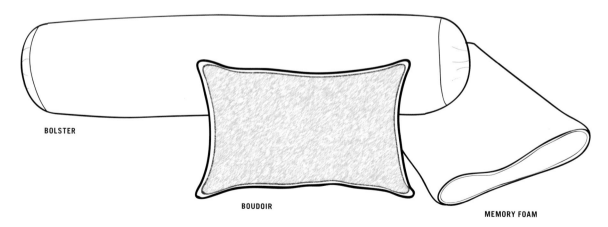

BOLSTER

BOUDOIR

MEMORY FOAM

A SYSTEM FOR DELIVERING THE PERFECT PILLOW.

Almost like a silver platter, the Pillow Butler®
requires the Pillow Menu Delivery and Storage
System to deliver the perfect pillow to each guest.

Pillow Butler®

Notes from a bedmaking journey

A BED SKIRT or a box spring wrap might be chosen to enhance the look of a bed. The box spring wrap encircles the box spring, offering a contemporary look. A bed skirt can become a housekeeper's nightmare, as the bed skirt tends to shift and move when tucking the sheets. For the final appearance to be top-notch, the bed skirt should be half an inch above the floor or carpet—it should not touch the floor or carpet.

To prevent the bed skirt from moving, you can use upholstery screws at the head of the bed to hold the bed skirt in place. The upholstery screws should be placed at least ten inches away from the corners of the head of the bed in order to prevent the housekeepers and bedmakers from injuring their fingers. However, if you have pets or young children, it is not advisable to use the screws, as they may get misplaced when rotating the box springs.

Another method is to use an adhesive piece at the head of the bed to fasten the bed skirt to the box spring. Since you will be rotating the box spring every quarter, the adhesive piece needs to be fastened to both the top and bottom of the upper surface of the box spring.

Bed skirts and box spring wraps are generally made of fabric that can be dry-cleaned or laundered. They should be cleaned at least every two to three months (depending on occupancy). This is an ideal project for the hotel's deep-cleaning team. Needless to say, the bed skirt must be checked daily by the housekeeper and should be replaced if stains or dirt are found. Nothing is more disturbing than a crushed, dirty bed skirt.

TYPES OF BED SKIRTS

Bed skirts should be constructed with a five-inch hem of fabric on a flat form so that you still see the same fabric if the mattress moves.

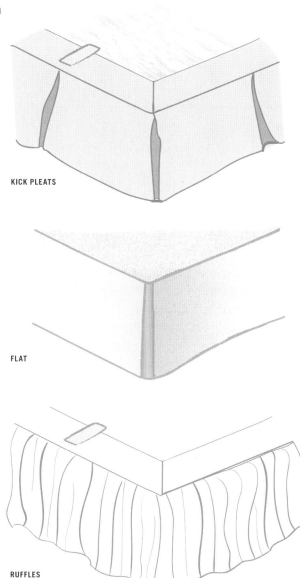

KICK PLEATS

FLAT

RUFFLES

Home Tip: Use a box spring cover instead of a bed skirt for a more contemporary look.

THERE IS NO DIFFERENCE between a comforter and a duvet. The comforter/duvet is the insert that goes into a cover, similar to the concept of a pillow going into a pillowcase.

The composition of a comforter/duvet is similar to the fill of a pillow; the choice is yours. When selecting a comforter, you will want to consider the type of fill, the weight, the size, and the covering, all of which may depend on the geographical location of your hotel. The comforter/duvet selected needs to fit a summer, fall, winter, or all-season environment.

Typically, the fill used in comforters/duvets is composed of down, feathers, or a combination of the two, although there are down alternatives made from hypoallergenic fabrics. Down is the cluster found on the underside of a goose or duck, composed of soft, fine strands stemming from a central point. As they interlock, they trap air, which keeps you warm. Feathers, on the other hand, are the outer plumage. They have a quill and are flatter than down, as well as thicker. Generally, the more down, the fluffier and softer the comforter; the more feathers, the firmer the comforter.

The weight of a comforter/duvet is determined by its fill power, which is the volume of an ounce of down. Down comforters come in several different weights to suit the needs of every sleeper, from light or summer weight to heavy or winter weight options. Consider the room temperature and whether windows will be open generally or sealed shut. Unless you or your guests sleep particularly hot or cold, we usually recommend a fall weight comforter.

The size of your comforter/duvet depends on the size of your bed, as well as the desired drop. They come in standard sizes including:

- twin: 63" x 88"
- full / queen: 88" x 94"
- king: 106" x 94"

The covering (ticking) of the comforter/duvet matters. The fabric should be soft but down proof in order to prevent the down and feathers from poking through or escaping.

Another major factor is the laundering of the comforter/duvet. Test wash the comforter/duvet prior to making the selection for your hotel. We recommend you add dryer balls, tennis balls, or clean, white sneakers to the dryer when drying feather and down products. Dryer balls are small, round fabric softeners; they take the stiffness out of bedding and open the fibers to bring back the loft/fluff in the bedding.

COMFORTER/DUVET COVERS

SELECTION:
- There are many styles of comforter/duvet covers. The comforter/duvet cover you select can give your bed a modern look.
- Cover designs vary and include: embroidery, dobby, jacquard, plain, striped,

printed, flanged, and piped.

- The thread count of the cover should play a large role in your choice of cover, as this is what gives the bed its luxurious feel. The life of the cover will be determined by the par in circulation and the laundering process, as well as wear and tear of the fabric. When a bed is made, the duvet cover will take up 90 percent of the bed's surface, so it should be wrinkle-free, smooth, and pleasing to the eye. The cover should look inviting.

CONSTRUCTION:

Comforter/duvet covers can be constructed to close in a number of ways, including:

- Overlay closure constructed with an envelope flap at the bottom, which can be tucked in to secure the comforter. Make sure the envelope flap on the comforter/duvet cover is at least fifteen inches in length so that the comforter/duvet stays firmly in the cover.
- Open sack, which leaves the bottom of the cover open. Make sure the sack is sewn with ten to eighteen inches on each side, so that the comforter is framed within the cover.
- Closed cover, which is constructed to close with zippers, Velcro, or buttons.

All three of these options can be constructed with ties inside the comforter/duvet cover and corresponding loops on the comforter/duvet, as well as with hand holes on the sides of the cover to access ties and loops.

The style you select should be approved by the hotel laundry manager, as ironing a comforter/duvet cover is a tedious process. When using a flat iron (mangle) in a commercial laundry, the best style is the envelope flap.

Notes from a bedmaking journey

BEDSIDE MATS ARE sometimes referred to as turndown mats. These mats are placed on the floor next to the side of the bed. The slippers are placed on the mats so that guests can slide into their slippers as soon as they get out of bed. The turndown attendant on the evening shift lays the mat next to the bed and places the slippers on it. There are many designs of turndown mats; the popular ones are made of white fabric. For an upscale feel, you can have your logo or crest embroidered or woven on these mats.

Bed throws (also known as bed scarves) are typically picked by a designer who is passionate about a well-dressed bed. The scarves are removed from the beds at turndown. You can also use a chenille blanket at the foot of the bed. This gives the guests an extra layer if needed during the winter season. The cleaning frequency of bed throws is important: the special project team should change them on schedule. Be sure to select a fabric that can withstand commercial laundering.

Remember, you cannot compromise cleanliness. If your laundry budget does not allow you to dry-clean or wash the throws or bed scarves, it is best not to include them in your top of the bed package. Hopefully, your designers have dealt with this aspect at the preopening stage of your hotel. There is a price tag attached to every design element. The fancier the bed, the higher the cost of maintenance.

Hotel Tip: For bed throws and scarves, be sure to select a fabric that can withstand commercial laundering.

Notes from a bedmaking journey

*W*HEN YOU SLEEP on a properly made bed, it is heaven. This is all due to the bedmaker!

Now that you know all the components of a bed, as well as those on top of the bed, you can learn how to make a bed.

TO MAKE A BED WITH TWO SHEETS AND A COMFORTER/DUVET

STEP 1: Put on your gloves.

STEP 2: Check for any personal items left behind on the bed by the guest and follow your lost-and-found guidelines. If you see any insects, you must leave the room and follow the guidelines set by management.

STEP 3: Remove the decorative pillows and place them on a sofa or chair (never on the floor or carpet).

STEP 4: Strip the bed by removing the sheets, pillowcases, and duvet cover. Place in the linen hamper or cart.

STEP 5: Wipe and dust the headboard.

STEP 6: Remove your gloves.

STEP 7: Pick up clean linen and place them on the desk or chair.

STEP 8: Check the mattress pad to make sure it is free of debris and hair.

STEP 9: Check the bed skirt for stains.

STEP 10: BOTTOM SHEET: Stand on one side of the bed and spread the bottom flat sheet on the bed. Always start at the head of the bed. The center of the sheet should be aligned with the center of the headboard. Tuck the sheet under the mattress at the head of the bed, making sure the sheet covers the mattress at least two to three inches under the mattress. Make the hospital corner on the side of the bed, pull and tuck the sheet at the foot of the bed, and make the hospital corner on the same side at the foot of the bed.

Following are detailed steps for making the perfect hospital corner:

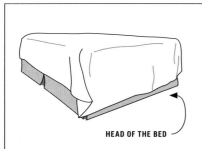

HEAD OF THE BED

10A. Pull the sheet at the head of the bed and cover the mattress tightly at the head of the bed.

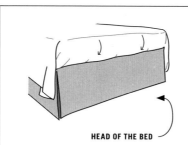

HEAD OF THE BED

10B. Lift the sheet hanging on the side of the bed twelve to fourteen inches from the corner of the bed and place on top of the mattress.

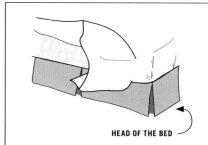

HEAD OF THE BED

10C. Pull and tuck the excess sheet under the mattress.

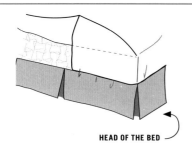

HEAD OF THE BED

10D. Drop the sheet you previously lifted from the top of the mattress against the side of the mattress and tuck it under the mattress. Note: The hospital corner fold will be forty-five degrees from the horizontal.

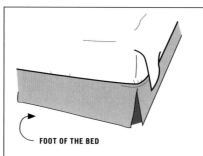

FOOT OF THE BED

10E. Repeat the previous instructions at the foot of the bed on the same side of the mattress.

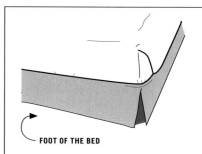

FOOT OF THE BED

10F: Repeat the hospital corners on the other side of the bed. Smooth the sheet with your palm to remove all creases.

STEP 11: SECOND SHEET: The second sheet is placed wrong side up with the edge at the end of the mattress with the headboard. Whip the sheet while spreading it in order to remove any creases. Center the sheet with the center of the headboard. The drop on either side of the mattress should be equal. Make the hospital corners at the foot of the bed.

STEP 12: COMFORTER/DUVET: Place the comforter/duvet insert
into the cover according to one of the following methods:

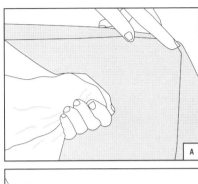

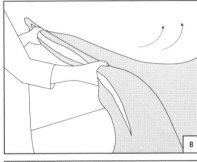

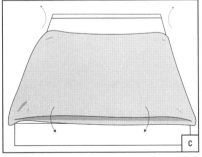

METHOD 1:

STEP A: Drape the comforter/duvet cover flat on the bed with the opening at the bottom of the bed. Hold the cover open with one hand. Hold the comforter/duvet insert at the top edges with the other hand and place the insert into the cover.

STEP B: While gripping the insert and cover together at the bottom, whip them into the air to move the insert into place in the cover.

STEP C: Adjust the cover properly on the bed by placing the top edge eight to ten inches from the headboard. Close the open end of the cover by placing the flap under the insert or by zipping the cover.

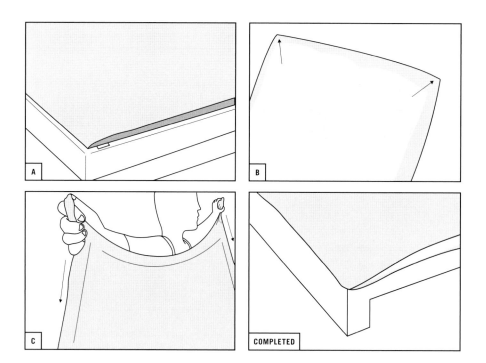

METHOD 2:

STEP A: Turn the comforter/duvet cover inside out and drape it flat on the bed with the opening at the bottom of the bed. The vendor label should sit at the bottom.

STEP B: Place the comforter/duvet insert on top of the cover.

STEP C: Slip both hands inside the opening of the cover at either side so that you can grab the insert and cover at the top edges from inside the cover. Lift the insert and cover together and turn the cover right side out around the insert just like a sock!

STEP 13: Fold the second sheet back over the duvet.

STEP 14: Place the pillows into the pillowcases.

STEP 15: Place the pillows on the bed according to your design standards. The following are different styles of pillow placements:

- Lay pillows flat on the bed and tier them.
- Place pillows upright vertically against the headboard one in front of the other.
- Angle pillows at a forty-five-degree angle to the headboard, one behind the other (see illustration on page 57.)

STEP 16: Place the decorative pillows according to your design standards.

STEP 17: Inspect the bed you have just made. There should be no lumps in the duvet cover, and the side of the mattress should be smooth and have perfect hospital corners. The second sheet should not peek from underneath the duvet cover on the side of the bed. Sweet dreams!

TO MAKE A BED WITH THREE SHEETS AND A BLANKET:

To make a bed with three sheets and a blanket (triple sheeting), repeat Steps 1 through 11 as shown and then:

STEP 12: Drape the blanket on the bed (with the label at the bottom) over the second sheet and place it eight to ten inches away from the headboard.

STEP 13: Place the third sheet (top sheet) on top of the blanket and extend it to the headboard.

STEP 14: Fold the top sheet under the blanket at the top of the bed.

STEP 15: Fold the second sheet (from the headboard) over the top sheet.

STEP 16: Tuck in the second and third sheets with the blanket between them on both sides of the mattress and at the foot of the bed. Make sure the hospital corners are at the side of the mattress (at the foot of the bed). When tucking the two sheets and the blanket, pull and tuck, and eliminate all creases and waves. If you pull the sheets and the blanket accordingly, you will have a lump-free bed.

After making the bed using the three sheets and blanket method, toss a quarter onto the bed. If you've made the bed nice and tight, the coin will flip. For a fancy three-sheeted bed, use a decorative hem on the second sheet so that, when you fold it over, the design will pop. A four- or five-inch design hem is required for this effect.

A rollaway bed is made either with three sheets and a blanket or two sheets and a comforter/duvet with a cover. The sheets, blankets, duvet, and comforter/duvet cover should be twin size.

When a housekeeper follows these training methods and takes pride in their job, the art of bed making will never be forgotten! Guests will be rewarded with *a great night's sleep.*

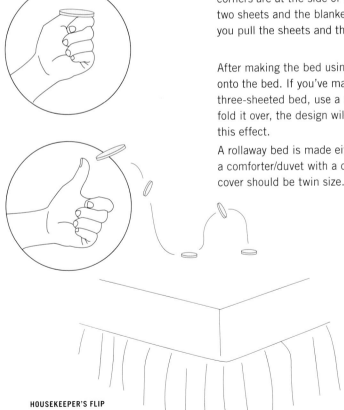

HOUSEKEEPER'S FLIP

HOT TOPICS FOR THE BED MAKING EXPERT

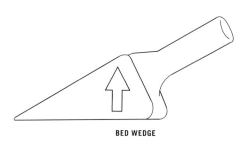

BED WEDGE

ALLERGIES. If a guest is allergic to feather products, you can provide them with hypoallergenic polyester pillows and cotton blankets.

BED BOARD. A thin piece of wood is placed between the mattress and box spring for guests who want a firmer bed. Have the bed board in twin, queen, and king sizes, readily available for your guests.

BED WEDGE. Use a bed wedge (pictured), a block of wood or hard plastic with a handle that can be placed underneath the mattress on the side of the bed when tucking the sheets. This allows you to refrain from lifting the mattress.

CELEBRATE. Housekeeping teams' successes should be celebrated in grand style with:

- pre-shift meetings for open communication
- a health and wellness stretching program
- monthly safety team celebrations
- monthly themed departmental meetings
- quarterly "Celebrate Our Success" meetings
- annual International Housekeepers Week celebrations:
  - poster contest
  - towel-folding contest
  - Inspect My Room: partner with other departments
  - bed making challenge: challenge the other departments
  - sit down for lunch with GM
  - multicultural fashion show: make a video and show it at town hall meetings
  - pillow stuffing relay (pillow, pillow protector, pillowcase)
  - duvet stuffing relay (duvet, duvet protector, duvet cover)
  - towel folding art
  - Pillow of the Month (POM) Club: Monthly drawing in which an employee is selected to win pillows for their own personal use. A photograph of the winning individual and their pillow(s) is taken and posted in a communal area.

CRIBS. Crib mattresses should be protected, too, so a LilyPads® crib mattress pad should always be used. To make a crib, use only a fitted sheet. For safety reasons, you should not place anything else inside a crib. It is inadvisable to use bumpers. Have baby blankets for sale in your gift shop for guests to purchase in case they don't bring their own. If you want to provide this service, sell disposable blankets in a plastic bag. Cleanliness of these blankets is very important. These blankets are for one-time use only. The crib's fitted sheet should be changed daily in a hotel room.

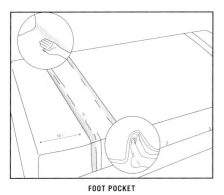

FOOT POCKET

FOOT POCKET. For a person with large feet, it is uncomfortable to sleep with the feet cramped down. If your budget allows, you can customize your sheets and have the manufacturer make a longer sheet (ten to thirteen inches longer). When you place this second sheet on the bed, make a pleat about ten inches from the end of the bed and make a pocket with the excess sheet in which the feet can move around freely. The foot pocket provides extra comfort, as it gives the feet extra room to be positioned upright with heels down for perfect comfort.

You can purchase extra-long king beds for big and tall guests. Although the width of extra-long kings is the same as that of standard kings, you will still need to purchase all new sheets, blankets, comforters/duvets, and covers. You can keep these extra-long beds in storage and assemble them in the room when they are requested. There should be an extra charge for this service. When on long vacations, tall guests who cannot sleep well in a hotel room will gladly pay this extra charge!

ONCE AROUND BED MAKING. A housekeeper's job is the most tedious in any hotel, so we must make every attempt to make their job easier. For once around bed making:

- Start at one side of the bed and handle the layers one by one.
- Tuck one side in according to the bed making guidelines, then move to the other side of the bed and handle the layers.
- The sheets must be "whipped" and accurately aligned for this procedure to work.
- Finally, place the comforter/duvet in the cover and drape on the bed.

SAFETY! Bed making can be dangerous for workers' backs if you do not train your team members properly. Make a video of your best bedmaker and use it as a training tool. A housekeeper should never attempt to flip or rotate a mattress or box spring alone. This assignment should be done in pairs and is best handled by the deep-cleaning crew.

When a housekeeper follows these training methods and takes pride in their job, the art of bed making will never be forgotten! Guests will be rewarded with *a great night's sleep.*

Tip: Our "Roll Into a Perfectly Made Bed" video, available on YouTube, offers a step-by-step tutorial demonstrating the art of making a bed.

Home Tip: You can make your bed like this at home, but don't stress—you don't have to! The most important part about making the bed is making sure the linens are refluffed and that air has circulated through them. This will give your bed a fresher and cleaner feel—which is one of the things people love about hotel beds anyway. Textiles need to breathe. If you would like, you can simply throw the comforter in the air and let it land on the bed. Your bed is your personal space and can be your own personal work of art.

*T*URNDOWN SERVICE (evening housekeeping service) is customary for luxury hotels; however, it is provided on request by many other hotels. The turndown attendant typically will perform this job function between six and nine o'clock in the evening. The ideal time to enter the room is when the guest is out enjoying hotel services. Depending on the size and extent of the room and its décor, a perfect turndown should take between six and ten minutes to complete.

This evening service pampers guests and prepares their beds for *a great night's sleep*. It is special, as it is something your guests do not get at home. It is meant to spoil them, adding to a guest's loyalty to the hotel brand. If you embrace the "one guest at a time" mentality, every guest will feel special and wanted. No matter how large your hotel, you can still treat every guest as if they are the only guest in the hotel. This is what gives your brand an edge!

The turndown card placed on the nightstand should be creative and should not be the same every day. Have seven cards printed, one for each day of the week. It is best to change the cards every six months so that returning guests do not receive the same message with every stay.

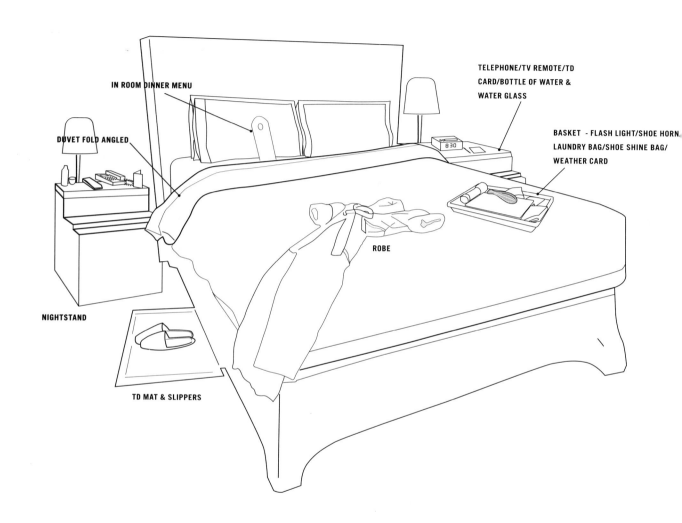

IN ROOM DINNER MENU

TELEPHONE/TV REMOTE/TD
CARD/BOTTLE OF WATER &
WATER GLASS

DUVET FOLD ANGLED

BASKET - FLASH LIGHT/SHOE HORN,
LAUNDRY BAG/SHOE SHINE BAG/
WEATHER CARD

ROBE

NIGHTSTAND

TD MAT & SLIPPERS

STANDARD TURNDOWN

TURNDOWN SERVICE

IN THE BATHROOM:

- Clean the tub/shower, if needed.
- Replace used towels (follow your hotel's green program).
- Replace the bath mat/rug if it is wet or dirty; fluff the bath rug to remove footprints.
- Remove trash from the wastebasket; replace the liner.
- Clean the sink, if needed; remove fingerprints left on the mirror.
- Replace used drinking glasses.
- Arrange the toiletries neatly on the vanity; use a special liner.
- Repoint facial tissue.
- Replenish amenities (soap/shampoo/conditioner/lotion). Follow your hotel's standard.
- Replace shaving towel, if needed.
- Check and clean the toilet, if dirty. Repoint the toilet tissue.

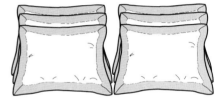

UPRIGHT-STRAIGHT

IN THE BEDROOM:

- Check the patio and remove dishes. Clean the ashtray.
- Call in-room dining (room service) to remove dishes, glasses, trays, etc.
- Return the iron and board to the closet.
- Turn down the bed by removing the decorative pillows and throws (place them on the closet shelf). Rearrange the pillows in one of the following illustrated positions:
  - Upright – straight.
  - Upright – angled.
  - Flat – one on top of the other.
- Top sheets and comforter/duvet are folded back for guests to snuggle in easily. Tighten the bottom sheet (pull and tuck). Bedsheets and cover may need to be changed, if wet or dirty.
- Robes are draped at the foot of the bed (or left on the robe hook in the bathroom).
- Turndown mat is placed beside the bed (use two mats if two guests are

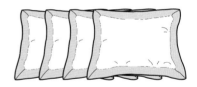

UPRIGHT-ANGLED

FLAT (ONE ON TOP OF ANOTHER)

occupying the room).

- Slippers are placed on the turndown mat facing away from the bed (to make it easier for the guest to wear the slippers when they wake up in the morning).

- The turndown amenity is placed on the nightstand or on the fold of the comforter/duvet and could be any of the following: chocolate, cookie, aromatic sachet, facial mist, a poem or inspirational message, weather card, hotel news, signature amenity, bottled water, etc.

- If bottled water is being offered, a drinking glass on a coaster should be placed on the nightstand.

- Set the TV/radio on a light music channel, and place the TV remote and TV card on the nightstand.

- Replenish ice in the ice bucket.

- Replace used glasses, napkins, stirrer sticks, etc.

- Guest clothing should be neatly handled (folded or hung) and shoes realigned and "paired."

- Magazines and newspapers should be neatly straightened. Use a bookmark to close an "open" book.

- Replenish stationery and collateral (i.e., printed marketing materials).

- Remove trash from the wastebasket and replace the liner.

- Close the patio door and close all drapes and sheers.

- Inspect the bedroom and the bathroom one final time to ensure that no detail was missed.

- Leave on only one light (next to the bed) and switch off all other lights. In a suite, the foyer light should be on "dim" setting.

- If a privacy sign or a "Do Not Disturb" sign is visible, never knock or enter the room. Leave a voice mail or slip a card under the door to inform the guest that you acknowledged their wish for privacy and did not offer the evening service.

ADDED TOUCHES FOR SPECIAL OCCASIONS:

You can design a special turndown for any occasion; the turndown amenity can be customized to create a certain ambiance. The turndown card should be customized for the occasion with special poems, verses, or stories. These touches are not limited to hotel guests; they work just as well at home.

ANNIVERSARY. Monogrammed or embroidered towels, bathrobes, and pillowcases.

BABYMOON. Leave a card with baby names on the nightstand.

EASTER. Towel animals such as a bunny on the nightstand will delight children.

FATHER'S DAY. A monogrammed chocolate celebrating dad might be appropriate.

HAPPY BIRTHDAY. Customize a birthday card and balloons.

HONEYMOON. Rose petals can be scattered on the carpet leading from the entry door to the bed, on the bed, and in the bathtub. A picture taken at the wedding ceremony or during the marriage proposal can be placed on the nightstand in a special frame. Inspirational poems can be placed on the nightstand. Monogrammed pillows can be offered.

MERRY CHRISTMAS/HAPPY HOLIDAYS. Holiday turndown cards, one for each of the seven days prior to Christmas.

MOTHER'S DAY. A special poem appreciating mothers and a flower can be placed in the room.

NEW YEAR'S EVE. Offer a pocket calendar for the new year.

THANKSGIVING. Create a poem for the season.

VALENTINE'S DAY. Rose petals can be scattered on the bed and in the bathtub. Place a single red rose on the bed.

OTHER UNIQUE SERVICES

To make a guest's or a loved one's sleep even more special, consider the following:

REJUVINATION. Offering *a great night's sleep* and refreshing awakening, this package includes luxurious Tiara Silks® charmeuse pillowcases with natural properties that nourish your skin's moisture and oils, and scent sachet aromatherapy blends of herbs and flowers that enhance your guests' ability to relax and dream.

EYESDOWN. Offer an eyesdown™ eye mask for those who enjoy sleeping in the dark.

DOG BED. Welcome pets with doggie treats, bowls, toys, and a doggie down™ blanket. Don't forget the doggie welcome note.

Notes from a bedmaking journey

CLEAN, CRISP, AND WELL-PRESSED linens are essential for a bed to look inviting! The laundry facility can be either onsite or offsite. If you opt for an onsite laundry facility, you will have more control over the quality of linens, and the par needed for linens, robes, bath mats, and towels will be less. If an offsite laundry facility handles your laundering daily, accountability and quality are of paramount importance. The number of par needed depends on the company's occupancy level, green program, volume of soiled linen/terry, and number of deliveries per week. In certain cities, the laundry facilities will not operate daily, so you will need to have a higher par of each item.

An in-house laundry manager should track productivity daily as follows:

- pounds cleaned per hour
- number of units (sheets, pillowcases, duvet covers, etc.) processed in the ironer per shift or by laundry attendant
- number of units processed in the towel folder per shift or by laundry attendant
- total number of pounds washed and processed per day

If the laundry facility is offsite, billing will be either by units processed with varied cost per type of towel, sheet, pillowcase, robe, etc. or by cost per pound (typically one flat rate regardless of type of terry item or linen).

It is imperative that rejected linen be accounted for regularly. Linens/terry should be picked up by the laundry facility daily, and the clean linen delivered should be verified by the laundry attendant. When paying by the pound, the laundry bins and hampers of linens/terry should be weighed and verified. If payment is by pieces, preset bundles should be accounted for.

The use of RFID (radio frequency identification) tags/chips has become very popular in the hotel industry. Sewn onto items, the RFID tags work by using radio frequency. This method helps with inventory management, as it eliminates the need to count every single item in inventory. It helps the hotelier keep their finger on the pulse of the asset. By leveraging the latest technology, you can control inventory tracking and make it more efficient. The cost of the tag will depend on the type, application, and order quantity. RFID tags/chips also serve the same purpose as woven sewn labels by helping to classify size, color coding, and branding. RFID eliminates the time spent on counting piece by piece daily or at month-end inventory. The old system of using barcodes or physically counting items has now become obsolete!

For a housekeeper to be content with their job responsibilities, an adequate supply of linens is a must. Be sure to replenish your par regularly and according to occupancy and set budget. When ordering linens, the lead time is crucial, especially if items are manufactured overseas. Be on top of your "linens game," have a well-organized linen closet, and maintain your number of par. Never run out of linens, as this will hurt your daily productivity and the morale of your operations.

ORE AND MORE HOTELS today are going green. Going green demonstrates a commitment to sustainability by your hotel. It also saves money by lowering laundry costs and increasing productivity (number of rooms cleaned per housekeeper). The goal is to reduce the cleaning industry's impact on the environment. Green cleaning is cleaning to protect our health without harming the environment.

When going green, you should:

- Seek volunteers to form a green team for your property.
- Design a feasible program.
- Get the buy-in of your team members.
- Get the approval of your ownership/management.
- Outline the program with easy-to-read captions.
- Design in-room collateral (i.e., printed marketing material) to educate your guests.
- Inform your laundry company of your program.
- Pilot the program on one floor and monitor it for a month.
- Set a kick-off date for the entire property.
- Inform the entire hotel at a town hall meeting.
- Continue monitoring the program.

One green initiative is changing linens in occupied rooms only when requested by guests. This eliminates the automatic daily changing of linens. The guest decides when they want their linens changed. Design a card specifically for your hotel and request that the guest place the card on the pillow if they wish for the linens (sheets/pillowcases) to be changed. The comforter/duvet cover should be changed only at checkout or if it is soiled.

A different method is to inform the guest (via the in-room collateral) that their sheets and pillowcases are changed on the third day (after two nights), but if they wish to have them changed daily, they are welcome to press a corresponding button on the in-room phone.

Many hotels, including the luxury market, have green programs in place. It is worth the effort to benchmark a hotel in your competitive set and learn their system prior to embarking on your own. Be informed—knowledge is power!

When a bed is remade as a green bed, the housekeeper should remake the bed with the existing sheets/pillowcases and pull and tuck the sheets back in place. If needed, the pillows should be straightened and fluffed. However, if the sheets or pillowcases are wet, stained, or soiled, they must be changed.

If you have a green program in place, your occupancy numbers should be monitored closely. Your daily staffing needs to be adjusted to reflect the number of green rooms; work assignments for housekeepers will be increased when there are green rooms, since bed making will be quicker. Loading the cart will also take less time due to the smaller number of sheets/pillowcases needed to be loaded.

Monitoring guest room cleanliness may become more difficult with a green program in place. The appearance of the bed may not be perfect, and the stains on the sheets may become too soiled for the laundry. However, your laundry cost will decrease, as you will have less soiled linens during occupied days. Because your chute operation will be easier during occupied days, staffing needs to be decreased accordingly. The number of linen hampers needed for soiled linens will shrink as well.

One major housekeeping change is the turndown service. When you turn down a green bed, the appearance will not be the same as a bed turned down with fresh linen. For turndown of a green bed, change the pillowcases daily, even if you don't change the sheets. Think about it—you still have a green bed!

There are many advantages in having a green program, but quality can slip if it is not monitored closely. The two main criteria for this program to be successful are the team member buy-in and the guests' happiness sleeping on a green bed. Supporting local communities with a percentage of the savings of your green bed program will encourage hotel guests to utilize the green program and provide great recognition of your hotel brand.

Warning: This harmless joke is to be played only on friends at home and never in your professional capacity as a housekeeper.

SINCE AT THIS POINT in the book you are a skilled bed maker, there is no need to review the way in which a normal bed is made. That is important, since the short-sheeted bed must appear normal to the person who is the subject of the joke.

The bottom part of the bed is made as usual. Things change once you are ready to place the flat sheet. Instead of tucking the flat sheet at the foot of the bed and leaving it open at the head of the bed, you will tuck the flat sheet at the head of the bed, smooth it halfway down the bed, and then fold it back up to the head of the bed. Place the blanket, duvet, or top sheet on top and tuck it in at the foot of the bed as you would normally do. Then fold the flat sheet back over the blanket so it appears as if it is open at the head of the bed and tucked in at the foot of the bed as usual. Place the comforter and pillows as usual.

When the subject lifts the covers to slide into the bed, their feet will only go as far as the point at which you folded the flat sheet back up at the middle of the bed.

Be on guard.

Fun Tip: Use newspaper instead of a mattress pad! The joke is now complete!

Notes from a bedmaking journey

ENDLESS POSSIBILITIES. I first saw them as a child in the tangram, the old Chinese puzzle where you take seven geometric shapes and build them into all kinds of larger shapes. You can make a square, or you can make any letter of the alphabet or any number zero through nine, but the possibilities go beyond that. I quickly became fascinated by everything that could be done with these geometric shapes and patterns, and this fascination followed me into a career in textiles and fashion.

Early in my career, I discovered that geometric variety could be combined with my other passion for fabric, in the design of pillows. Fabric is more important to our lives than we often realize, and pillows can serve more purposes than sleeping—in particular, they are the perfect accent or decoration for any room. If you change the fabric on a pillow, you can change the energy of an entire room. I began developing pillows in a variety of shapes for a variety of purposes.

I started Down Etc and opened the company's showroom in San Francisco in 2001. In the beginning, I was creating geometric pillow forms and manufacturing, cutting, and sewing decorative pillow covers. I developed original pillow forms—beach balls, boxes, triangles, cubes, cones, and bolsters of all sizes. I could trace this back to the influence of the tangram—putting pieces together in different ways.

Since then, Down Etc has grown into an international company and a leading supplier of bed linens and pillows for major hotels, boutique hotels, cruise ship lines, and other luxury chains around the world. We are a purpose-driven business: our goal is to offer everyone *a great night's sleep*. This book shares that purpose.

For those in the hospitality industry, you now know all of the basics for maintaining a high-quality brand standard. Your guests will be able to get *a great night's sleep* when they are traveling. For those at home who want *a great night's sleep* for themselves, you don't have to strive for hotel quality—the key is to make your bed and your bedroom your own space for relaxation and rejuvenation based on what appeals to your senses.

We have the same philosophy at Down Etc We have found that the best way to engage guests is to appeal to all of their senses at the same time rather than focus on one or two. It's a great way to make a first impression. When you walk through the front door of the Down Etc showroom, we welcome you by offering you the opportunity to wash your hands and giving you a cup of tea. Beautiful music is playing and a scented candle is burning. You are surrounded by positive energy and your senses are engaged. Then we ask how you are sleeping.

A great night's sleep can be aided by these types of rituals—taking off your shoes as soon as you enter the house, washing your hands when you come into a space, preserving the bedroom as a space for sleeping with no electronics. Your home, and your bedroom in particular, should be a sanctuary where you can leave the outside world behind and relax, rejuvenate, and recalibrate. We wish you *a great night's sleep*.

IMPROPER INVENTORY OR LINEN DISTRIBUTION. Check your linen closets in the morning and make sure the par is maintained daily. Know your par on hand and monitor the distribution of linens onsite. Monthly full linen inventory is a must. Know your linen loss per room. Know your linen purchase cost per room. Replenish inventory on a regular basis. Adequate supply of linens is a housekeeper's life! Habitual lack of linen will result in high turnover of housekeepers, and the department will go downhill.

LACK OF A DEEP CLEANING PROGRAM. It is important to check the frequency of changing pillow protectors, mattress pads and encasements, bed skirts, bed scarves, decorative pillows, etc.

LACK OF KNOWLEDGE. Be knowledgeable; be prepared to answer questions from guests and team members regarding the bed and the "top of bed" at your hotel.

LACK OF TRAINING. Train your staff after they attend the hotel's orientation. Never remove a team member from the training session to service rooms. Always let a new hire complete at least two weeks of hands-on training.

NOT READING THE GUEST COMMENTS. Follow up on every opportunity. Why is the bed uncomfortable? Why are the sheets turning gray? Why is the quality so poor? Why are the sheets so wrinkled? Why does the duvet cover have holes, tears, or rips? Why are there black marks on so many sheets? Why are the sheets turning yellow? And so on.

OUT-OF-STOCK ITEMS. Send your purchase orders on time and follow up on delivery dates and hold the vendor accountable when items are not delivered on time.

OVERLOADING A NEW HIRE. Start with six rooms per day and gradually increase the quantity.

POOR ATTITUDE OF THE TRAINER. The trainer should have the best attitude in your department; he or she should be a model team member.

SHORTCUTS. Follow the bed making steps; sheets must be changed according to the hotel's standards. Not changing sheets at checkout is a deadly sin!

Skipped quality check. Work closely with your laundry manager, be supportive, and keep a close watch on the stain removal process, as well as the reclaim process.

SLOPPY ROOM INSPECTIONS. Inspect your guest rooms on a regular basis. It is the job of the chief housekeeping officer to check that the beds are being made properly and the quality of linen is perfect. If you are not seen on the floors, your management team will follow your lead! Be present, be seen, and be approachable.

YOU DO NOT LIKE YOUR JOB! Love what you do and do what you love! If you love your job, you will be loyal to the hotel you work for and its brand standards. If you don't truly like the housekeeping profession, it will damage your associates, employees, department, hotel, and eventually yourself. Be ahead of the curve! Network with fellow professionals. Be a mentor for the next generation.

In order to provide your guests with the best service, make sure your staff can answer the following questions:

1. I had a great night's sleep. Where can I buy these products for my home?
2. What is the TC (thread count) of the sheets on which I slept?
3. What are your cleaning procedures?
   a. How often are the linens, blankets, comforters/duvets, or bedspreads cleaned and how is that done?
   b. How do you clean the pillows, and how often?
   c. How often do you replace the pillows?
   d. Do you have hypoallergenic pillows?
   e. Do you disinfect the cribs after each guest's use?
   f. Do you clean the decorative pillows and how often?
4. Do you provide cribs and/or rollaway beds?
5. Have you ever had bedbugs in your hotel?
6. I am allergic to detergents; can you wash my sheets and/or towels in hot water only?
7. What is the coil count in the mattress?
8. How old is the mattress? How often do you clean your mattresses?
9. May I have brand new linens on my bed?
10. Do you have a dehumidifier?
11. How often are the carpets in the guest rooms shampooed?
12. I do not like the duvet. May I have a cotton blanket instead, and would you three-sheet my bed?
13. I want a simple bed with king-size sleeping pillows. Can you remove all decorative pillows?
14. I would prefer a firmer bed. May I have a bed board placed under the mattress?
15. When was your hotel last rated by AAA (diamonds) and Forbes (stars)?

Notes from a bedmaking journey

Knowledge Is Power

[B]

bed board
A thin sheet of wood placed between the mattress and the box spring.

bed frame
The contraption that carries the mattress and box spring.

bed skirt
A decorative piece used to cover the box spring and legs of the bed; it fits between the mattress and box spring and hangs to the floor; a.k.a. dust ruffle.

bed throw
A bed scarf at the foot of the bed that has decorative value.

bedspread
A bedspread is a bed cover with sides that cover the mattress; a.k.a. spread.

bottom sheet
A bed linen with a hem that is the first sheet placed on the mattress; could be a fitted sheet as well.

box spring
A foundation made using some type of wood with an outer covering of fabric, placed under a mattress for support.

[C]

coil count
Number of coils in a mattress.

coil gauge
The thickness of a coil in a mattress.

comforter
A quilted bedcover filled with feathers, down, and/or other natural or manmade fibers; available in a variety of weights; a.k.a. duvet.

comforter cover
A sack-like covering, with three closed sides and one open side, in which a comforter fits; overlay closure is usually around fifteen inches and uses ties, zippers, buttons, or Velcro; a.k.a. duvet cover.

construction

invisible baffled box construction
The ticking of the comforter/duvet is sewn within the interior walls that separate the down or down alternatives into box-shaped compartments; this displaces the down evenly throughout the comforter; the baffled seams have a height of one and one-quarter inches, which keeps the two layers of ticking lifted apart to allow air to flow and the comforter to maintain its loft.

sewn-through construction
The ticking of the comforter/duvet is sewn through to separate the down or down alternatives into box-shaped compartments.

coverlet
Traditionally a lightweight, woven spread used on the top of the bedding; can be big enough to hang down the sides of a bed or just cover the top of the bed so that the bed skirt or bed frame is exposed.

[D]

day bed
A seat large enough for a small child to lie upon.

decorative pillows
Pillow accessories for the top of bedding.

down
The cluster found on the underside of a goose or a duck (waterfowl); the clusters of soft, fine strands stem from a central point. As they interlock, they trap air, which keeps you warm.

Generally, the more down, the fluffier and softer the pillow or comforter; the more feathers, the firmer the pillow or comforter.
and feathers.

drop
Describes how far the bedcover falls from the top of the mattress.

duvet
A quilted bedcover filled with feathers, down, or other natural or manmade fibers; available in a variety of weights; a.k.a. comforter.

duvet cover
Sack-like covering with three closed sides and one open side that fits over a comforter; the overlay closure is usually around fifteen inches and uses ties, zippers, buttons, or Velcro; a.k.a. comforter cover.

duvet protector
Similar to a pillow protector; often used like a duvet cover for triple sheeting, but it is not washed daily.

[E]

embroidery
Decorative, ornamental needlework stitches used to dress up a base fabric; can be machine woven or done by hand.

encasement
Protector for the mattress or box spring. See onguard!®

Euro pillow
A twenty-six-by-twenty-six-inch pillow. Custom sizes are available.

Euro sham
A decorative casing for square pillows often placed behind the sleeping pillows as a backdrop or on top of sleeping pillows as a coordinated set with a comforter/duvet cover.

[F]

fill power
The standard that measures the number of cubic inches filled by an ounce of down. The more space an ounce of down takes up, the more warmth it provides. This is because the more space it occupies, the more air it entraps (the air provides the warmth).

fill weight
The ounces of fill in a comforter/duvet or pillow; this is determined by what you want the overall product to look and feel like.

fitted sheet
Bed linen with elastic all the way around.

flat sheet
Bed linen with hem.

fluff
To shake the pillow to loosen the fill and provide loft.

foot pocket
Placement of second sheet to create room for the foot.

[G]

green bed
A bed made with sustainability in mind.

[H]

hand
A term for how fabric feels to the touch.

hand holes
Used for housekeepers to easily insert a comforter/duvet into a cover; seven to nine inches in length and sewn on the sides of a cover ten inches from the top of the cover.

headboard
A board or panel that sits at the head of a bed.

[I]

in-wall bed
A bed placed vertically into a wall pocket when not in use.

invisible zipper
A hidden zipper on a pillow or duvet protector or decorative pillow closure.

[J]

jacquard
A weave that creates an intricate, textured pattern within the fabric; examples include tapestries, brocades, and damask fabrics.

[L]

Lily Pads®
A waterproof, motionless, noiseless, absorbent, washable, breathable mattress protector manufactured as a pad with anchor bands or a full, fitted skirt; an incontinence care sleep solution.

loft
Puffiness of a comforter or pillow; a result of having enough air flowing through the comforter.

loops
Pieces of fabric attached to the corners of a comforter/duvet that are tied to corresponding ties attached to the cover in order to hold the comforter in place in the cover. See ties.

linens
Bedsheets, pillowcases, shams, pillow and duvet protectors, and comforter/duvet covers.

[M]

matelassé
A soft, jacquard-woven fabric with a quilted, puckered surface appearance that adds dimension and texture; used most often in coverlets.

mattress
A cushioned or upholstered piece of furniture containing coils, which is made to be slept on. The number and gauge of the coils determines the firmness and enhances the quality of the mattress.

mattress pad
Used as the protective layer on top of the mattress and mattress topper; a.k.a. bed pad. See Lily Pads®.

mattress topper
An extra layer on top of the mattress.

memory foam
Polyurethane foam that changes its shape in reaction to body temperature, thereby "remembering" the shape of the person using it and providing more comfortable, body-contouring support.

[O]

once around bed making
A bed making technique that prevents one from having to run around the bed multiple times.

onguard!®
Bed bug proof (dust mite proof), breathable mattress and box spring encasement.

par
Quantity of linens needed for a hotel operation to cover all rooms. Par level is the number of par maintained by a hotel.

Pillow Butler®
A system allowing sleepers to select the pillow that is best for them.

pillow protector
Cover for the pillow with a zipper or overlay closure used to protect the pillow from stains and body fluids as you drool at night during sleep.

pillowcase
The cover for a pillow; a.k.a. pillow slip.

piping
A thin decorative trim used to finish a hem or seam, or as an outline; can be the same or contrasting fabric.

pockets
The corners of fitted sheets sized specifically to accommodate today's thicker mattresses.

rollaway bed
A movable bed on wheels; provided as an extra bed upon request; a.k.a. cot.

sateen
A luxury fabric woven very tightly using the satin weave technique, which imparts a subtle sheen and a soft, silky hand.

sham
A decorative covering for a pillow, often designed with trims, ruffles, flanges, or cording; normally placed in front of the pillows used for sleeping, which are covered with regular pillowcases.

sheet set
A complete set that includes a flat sheet, a fitted sheet, and two pillowcases.

shell
The outermost layer of fabric used to manufacture pillows, comforters, or mattresses; a.k.a. ticking.

sofa bed
A seat that can be pulled out to serve as a bed.

[T]

TC (thread count)
The number of vertical and horizontal threads per square inch of a woven fabric. Higher thread counts result in smoother, more durable fabric.

throw
A decorative blanket, sometimes called a bed scarf, placed at the foot of the bed.

ticking
The outermost layer of fabric used to manufacture pillows, comforters, or mattresses; a.k.a. shell.

ties
Strips of fabric attached to the corners of a comforter/duvet cover, which are tied to corresponding loops attached to a comforter/duvet to hold it in place. See loops.

top sheet
Bed linen with hem that is the last sheet placed on the bed.

triple sheeting
Making a bed with three sheets and a comforter/duvet or blanket.

trundle
The drawer base under a bed that pulls out for another bed.

[W]

whip
To unfold a clean sheet to commence bedmaking.

BE ONGUARD!® FOR BEDBUGS

With travel comes the threat of bedbugs. You may not be able to prevent bedbugs from hitchhiking into your hotel on your guests' luggage and clothing—or from a hotel to your home—but you can protect your box spring and mattress from infestation with the onguard!® collection. onguard!® encasements are made of polyester tightly woven to be anti-microbial, anti-allergen, flame retardant, and dust mite and bed bug proof. Contact us for sizes and immediate delivery options.

LILY PADS® LET YOU REST ASSURED

Protect mattress from perspiration, spills, and other accidents with Lily Pads®, the waterproof, motionless, soundless, and breathable mattress pad. The polyester nonwoven backing provides a waterproof barrier while the all-cotton twill top layer provides a soft and silky base for the bottom sheet. Contact us for sizes and immediate delivery options.

SERVE YOUR GUESTS THE PERFECT PILLOW

The Pillow Butler® is every hotel's solution to the pillow menu. It's a first-class pillow service and offers staff a pillow menu delivery, shelving, and storage system customized to your hotel's pillow selection. Contact us to learn more about this professional, hygienic pillow presentation and delivery system.

FOR OUR FURRY FRIENDS

doggie down™ is the perfect solution for pet friendly hotels! Made of a three-layer barrier fabric of polyester with a nonwoven back, doggie down™ is washable, waterproof, noiseless, and breathable and protects furniture and carpet from pet dander and accidents. It rolls up and wraps in removable Velcro bands for easy carrying and storage, and it is manufactured in any size or color to match any room's décor. Contact us for sizes and immediate delivery options.

MORE GREAT WAYS TO LET THEM SLEEP ON IT

down etc...•

Tel: 415-348-0084
Fax: 415-348-0085
Toll-Free: 866-down etc
info@downetc.com
www.downetc.com

83

START GETTING

A Great Night's Sleep

TONIGHT

GET THE RESOURCES YOU NEED TO LET EVERYONE YOU KNOW SLEEP ON IT!

FREE pillowcise™ GUIDE

Nothing makes the start of the day brighter after a perfect night's sleep than an invigorating full-body stretch. Our pillowcise™ video, available on YouTube, offers a step-by-step tutorial demonstrating these stretches.

FREE NEWSLETTER

Stay informed on cutting-edge industry solutions to housekeeping and bedding challenges. Sign up at www.downetc.com for our monthly newsletter for exclusive content.

FREE VIDEOS

Explore Down Etc's library of free educational videos to discover some unexpected ways to enhance your sleeping experience.

CONSULTATIONS

Give your housekeeping staff the opportunity to learn about the current industry standards while getting the tools to solve their most important or difficult problems. The Down Etc team, led by author Rebecca Litwin, will energize your team and give them the confidence to make it happen.

ASK THE PILLOW EXPERTS

Looking for some inspiration? Check out our blog, find answers to our most frequently asked questions, or ask us your specific questions at www.downetc.com.

down etc ...

Tel: 415-348-0084
Fax: 415-348-0085
Toll-Free: 866-down etc
info@downetc.com
www.downetc.com

85